YOUR KNOWLEDGE HAS VALUE

Bibliographic information published by the German National Library:

The German National Library lists this publication in the National Bibliography; detailed bibliographic data are available on the Internet at http://dnb.dnb.de .

Imprint:

Copyright © 2019 GRIN Verlag
Print and binding: Books on Demand GmbH, Norderstedt Germany
ISBN: 9783346033819

This book at GRIN:

https://www.grin.com/document/498656

Dickson Apraku

The legal classification of the armed conflict in Yemen

GRIN Verlag

GRIN - Your knowledge has value

Since its foundation in 1998, GRIN has specialized in publishing academic texts by students, college teachers and other academics as e-book and printed book. The website www.grin.com is an ideal platform for presenting term papers, final papers, scientific essays, dissertations and specialist books.

Visit us on the internet:

http://www.grin.com/

http://www.facebook.com/grincom

http://www.twitter.com/grin_com

1. INTRODUCTION

The situation in Yemen has now turned into an international debate and the mechanisms to deal with the situation have remained unanswered. The conflict began when the Yemeni protected against the President Ali Abduallah Salah with the aim of regime change due to the failure of the government to tackle the issues of poor economy, insecurity, corruption, and exclusive governance and low standard of living and many more. The situation has turned the country apart and the situation of violence is still remains unresolved since 2011.

In this regard, the present study intends to cover the historical framework of the situation in Yemen, the legal framework of the conflict, the scopes of armed conflicts, and how does International Humanitarian Law (IHL) classify the armed conflict in Yemen and lastly the legal conclusion.

2. HISTORICAL FRAMEWORK OF THE SITUATION IN YEMEN

The Republic of Yemen was established in 1990 in which the former Yemen Arab Republic in North and those of the former Peoples' Democratic Republic of Yemen in South were integrated.[1] The country first conducted their election in 1993 and due to the political challenges of the results ended up dividing the country. Thus, the peoples in Southern Yemen voted for the Yemeni Socialist Party (YSP) and those in Northern Yemen voted for the Islah Party (an Islamic group) and as well as the General People's Congress (GPC).[2] A study has shown that the situation of violence started when both parties, thus, the GPC and YSP were challenging the national election results. Both parties fought for a year and those in Southern Yemen were defeated. [3]

However, for the purpose of identifying, analysing and examining the IHL rules with regard to the conflict in Yemen, this study will not focus much attention on the past situation but rather it will stress upon the conflict that took place since 2004 to present.

Yemeni Government has been engaged in armed conflict since 2004 with organised armed groups such as Houthis that was established in 1990 and has geographically located itself in

---

[1] See Louise Arimatsu and Mohbuba Choudhury (2014), The Legal classification of the Armed Conflicts in Syria, Yemen and Libya. Page 20, also see www.chathamhouse.org.
[2] See ibid, page 20, para.3
[3] See ibid

Northern Yemen and is headed by Ansar Allah.[4] Since 2004 to 2011, the situation of violence reached a significant level of intensity, massive death toll roll, high rate of sexual violence especially against women and girls, killing of civilians population and government properties like houses, schools, hospital, mosques and military objectives were damaged.[5] These were as a result of economic discontent and sectarian divisions[6], however, President Saleh employed strong security measures to check an insurgency initiated by the Houthis,[7]this made the Houthis also to start demonstrations to overthrow President Saleh's government from power. The situation became worsened when the government forces used excessive force to suppress the demonstrations.[8]

Furthermore, due to the long period of the demonstration, this brought pressure on President Saleh to step down and hand over power to his deputy Addrabuh Mansour Hadi through the initiative of Gulf Corporation Council in late 2011.[9] In February 2012, Hadi was elected as a president of Yemen during their national election. Since he assumed office in 2012, his administration has been confronted with many challenges including political crisis and heavy protests in June 2014 against the cut of fuel subsidies happened in Northern Yemen controlled by the Houthis.[10]

In September 2014, the Houthis and their ally General People's Congress took control over the capital Sanaa and in a matter of a short period after taking over Sanaa had a dialogue with Hadi's government. This brought political stability until January 2015 when there was disagreement on the constitutional draft process which erupted violence again.[11]On 24 March 2015, President Hadi appealed to the United Arab Emirates (UAE), Saudi Arabia, Qatar, Bahrain, Kuwait and Oman for military intervention and to support his government to fight

---

[4] See the International Commission of Jurists, A Briefing paper (2018). Bearing the Brunt of war in Yemen: International law violations and their impact on the civilian population. Page3
[5] See Human Rights Watch report (2010), Yemen armed hostilities are referred to as the 'six wars'
[6] See ibid
[7] See Geneva Academy, Non-International Armed Conflicts in Yemen, also see http/www.rulac.org/browse/conlicts/non-international-armed-conflicts-in-yemen.
[8] See Human Rights Watch, World Report(2012)
[9] See the Gulf Corperation Council Initiative (Yemen), April 2011, para.4
[10] See ibid
[11] See Salah Arraf (2015), The Armed Conflict in Yemen: A complicated Mosak, Geneva Academy.

against the Houthis.[12]However, on 25 March 2015, Hadi fled to these countries and others for international intervention.[13]

Moreover, on this basis, the Saudi-led Coalition through the support of USA came to intervene in support of his government in order to help to fight against the Houthis and other organised armed groups such as AQAP, AAS and anti-Saleh militia groups. In this light, on 26 March 2015, the Saudi Arabia-led coalition conducted an airstrike on the Houthis and Houthis also responded by conducted ground operation against the Hadi forces.[14] Again, in March 2016, the U.S.A government provided logistics and intelligence support to the Saudi-led coalition to facilitate them to conduct hostilities against the Houthis.

Addition, Iran in the opposite side has claimed responsibility of the support and intervene the Houthis and the rebel forces to help them to fight against the government forces and the conflict escalated. [15]

3. LEGAL FRAMEWORK OF THE ARMED CONFLICT.

The applicability of the Law of Armed Conflict (LOAC) is dependent on the amount of degree the situation of violence existed[16] in a legal sense. Any situation of violence whose degree does not amount to an armed conflict is governed by international human rights law. However, IHL rules recognise only two situations where the LOAC that governs and these situations are: the international armed conflict (IAC) and a non-international armed conflict (NIAC).[17] An IAC is simply defined as an armed conflict between two or more states whiles the NIAC is defined as armed conflict between a state and one or more organised armed group(s).[18] The distinction of these situations of armed conflict is very significant in a sense that the applicability of the law of armed conflict (LOAC) depends on whether the nature of the armed of the conflict as to whether it falls under IAC or NIAC. In this light, the study shall proceed to elaborate these two concepts.

---

[12] See UN Document in 27 March 2015, S/2015/217
[13] See ibid s.Arraf (2017)
[14] See ibid
[15] See Ishan Jan, M.N and Lawan Haruna, A (2015), Saudi-led Military Intervention in Yemen and International Law. Page 7
[16] See the terms Law of Armed Conflict (LOAC) and International Humanitarian Law (IHL)
[17] See Louse Arimatsu and Mohbuba Choudhury (2014), page 3
[18] See ibid

(A) International armed conflict (IAC)

The applicable law that applies to IAC, in general, is found under common Article 2 of the Geneva Convention (1949). The textbox in common Article 2 has clearly stated that armed conflict may exist when there is an armed conflict between two or more of the high contracting parties[19] and this provision has further emphasized that armed conflict will remain international even if the state of the conflict is not recognised by one of the contracting parties. In lieu of this, the International Committee of the Red Cross (ICRC) their commentary to the Geneva Convention, they have claimed that the different situation that arises between two or more states and if it calls for the international community intervention, such situation of violence still remain IAC.[20] The ICRC has further argued that the situation of violence does not matter the degree of time in which it takes.[21]

(B) Non-International Armed Conflict (NIAC)

Generally, there is no absolute definition for NIAC but the applicable law that governing a NIAC is tagged to two instruments under the Treaty Law with the ad hoc Tribunals. The below are the two instruments: Common Article 3 of the Geneva Convention (CA3) and the Additional Protocol II (APII).[22] The CA3 claims to regulate conflicts between a state and non-state actors and it also deals with the internal situations but unlike the CA2, it claims to regulate those conflicts between two or more states.[23] Again, under Article 1 of APII, it identifies the situation of violence that does not reach the armed conflict threshold[24] and likewise, it's applied to CA3.

However, to be able to determine the existence of a NIAC, the International Criminal Tribunal for the Former Yugoslavia (ICTY) has vividly affirmed in a case of Prosecutor v.Tadic that a NIAC may exist when there is protracted armed conflict between a state and organised armed group(s).[25] In the light of this, studies have shown that there are two main key elements that constitute a NIAC namely the intensity of hostility and involvement of an

---

[19] See the Common Article 2 of the Geneva Convention(i-iv)
[20] See ICRC Commentary to Article 2 of the First Geneva Convention (1952)
[21] See ibid
[22] See ibid
[23] See Derek Jinks (2013), The Temporal Scope of application of International Humanitarian Law in Contemporary Conflict. Page 2
[24] See the Commentary to Article 1 of APII
[25] See Prosecutor v. Tadic, IT-94-1, 2 October 1995, para 4341.

organised armed group(s).[26] However, the study shall proceed to elaborate these two key elements that constitute a NIAC.

(i)   The Intensity of threshold (hostility)

A study has shown that in order to determine whether a situation of violence amounts to the intensity threshold, certain criteria should be met. For instance, in cases of Prosecutor v. Fatmir Limaj and Prosecutor v Haradinaj, the ICTY applied the test enumerated in the Tadic Jurisdiction decision to conclude that the level of intensity surrounding the armed conflict must meet certain factors such as, seriousness of attacks and its recurrences must be identified, the spread of violence over territory and over a period of time of the violence must be examined, whether there was an increase number of state forces, and whether various parties to the conflicts were able to take over the territory under their control, whether there was a mobilisation and the distribution of weapons among the various parties to the conflict, whether the conflict has called for relevant action by the United Nations Security Council and lastly whether any resolution(s) has been adopted to end the conflict.[27] However, for the purpose of determining the intensity of hostility, the above factors should be applied.

(ii)   The organisational element

In regard to the organisational element as a second criterion in determining a NIAC, a study has shown that the various groups must be organised or structured and must be armed to the degree that they have the capacity to exercise military activities or operations.[28] However, for the purpose of examining whether the organisation or the group has reached its threshold, for example in a case of Prosecutor v. Limaj, the ICTY has examined the following factors or elements that need to be met. They include, the organisation or the group should have internal regulations and have the commander instructing them, there should have headquarters, the group should have the ability to procure and the establishment of a military police must be identified, they should have designed zones for operation, availability of transports and they should have the ability to distribute arms or weapons, they should have uniforms and lastly the organisation should have other various equipment for operations.[29]

---

[26] See ibid
[27] See Prosecutor v. Fatmir Limaj (IT-03-66-T), 30 November 2005 and Prosecutor v. Haradinaj (IT-04-84-T), 3 April 2008.
[28] See ibid
[29] See Prosecutor v. Fatmir Limaj (IT-03-66-T), 30 November 2005

Having mentioned the legal framework of the armed conflict, the study shall proceed to answer the below question:

4. HOW DOES AN INTERNATIONAL HUMANITARIAN LAW (IHL) CLASSIFY THE ARMED CONFLICT IN YEMEN?

For the purpose to determine whether the conflict in Yemen is falling under IAC or a NIAC, the study shall examine the various factors. Thus, the intensity threshold, organisational structure, actors involved in the conflict and other cited cases.

Looking at the historical framework of the Yemen conflict, one could assert that the conflict escalated in between January and May 2011.[30] And obviously, many armed groups are involved in the conflict as stated above. There is some evidence that as at May 2011, there was an armed conflict between the Houthis and the government forces established in Saana where many civilians population were killed.[31] On the basis of the available information provided in the study's historical framework of the Yemen conflict, however, identify that the Houthis are a well-established organisation with a superior command structure. Secondly, Houthis were able to establish their own system of governance and managed to move the government forces established in Saana under their control, thirdly, they were able to distribute arms or weapons and other related military equipment. Fourthly, they were able to procure and provide military training to new members and finally, the Houthis were able to engage in a political negotiation with Hadi's government.

Therefore, on the basis of the above assessment and with regard to the IHL rules, it is showing clearly that the conflict reached the intensity threshold and in lieu of this the Houthis met the organisational requirement.

Moreover, some legal experts have argued that the IHL does not explicitly provide the guidance on whether the actors to the Yeman conflict such as Houthis is classified as Yemen State.[32] However, under international human rights perspective, Houthis do not meet the statehood criterion. Hence, they are classified as a non-state entity. Therefore, based on the enormous legal analysis highlighted in this study, the current situation of violence in Yemen

---

[30] See ibid
[31] See ibid
[32] See ibid

is an armed conflict between the Hadi's governments and organised armed group (Houthis) and therefore, non-international armed conflict is applicable.

But, interestingly, one could argue that the conflict in Yemen involved with multiple parallels and overlapping of NIAC in which CA3 is applied[33]on the basis of the issue arise in the Saudi-led Coalition and Iran interventions. Now, having stated that the conflict in Yemen is a NIAC, it is important to examine whether the intervention of Iran and Saudi-led Coalition can change the character of the conflict to which IHL is applied. Obviously, a NIAC mostly can change its nature to internationalised armed conflict when there is an excessive intervention of a third state.[34]

With regard to Iran intervention, albeit Iran in support of the Houthis to help them to fight against the Hadi's government forces met the internationalised criterion, thus, the support must be given to the rebel forces in order to determine effectively the fought between two or more states either directly or through an agent(s).[35] On the basis of this, for the purpose to determining the level of support or intervention to the organised armed group in order to change the nature of the conflict, the IHL rules have stipulated that a state which is intervening must exercise overall control over the hostilities of the armed group, secondly, the involvement must reach a certain degree that the hostilities of the organised armed group can be attributed to the intervening state. For example is a case of Prosecutor v. Tadic, the ICTY has claimed that for any conduct to be attributed to the state, the given state should not only exercise authority over those organised armed group but rather must also provide specific instructions to the group and this may be related to the performance of the acts being provided.[36]

Therefore, the study may claim that the fact that Iran is providing military weapons, training and financing the Houthis does not mean that hostilities of Houthis are attributable to Iran state because based on the available information, Iran does not exercise overall control over the Houthis and also Iran does not provide any specific instructions to the Houthis. However, it is showing clearly that the hostilities of Houthis cannot be attributed to Iran. Hence, the Iran intervention in support of the Houthis does not affect the character of NIAC in Yemen.

---

[33] See customary international law obligations that applicable to NIAC.
[34] See ibid Jinks, D (2003)
[35] See ibid
[36] See ibid

With regard to the Saudi-led Coalition intervention, one could claim that the support of the Yemeni government forces does not affect the nature of the conflict because the Saudi-led Coalition interventions do not meet above criteria of internationalised armed conflict based on the available information.[37] Thus, the Saudi-led coalition does not take overall control over the government forces neither given them specific instructions. Finally, on this basis, it is obvious that the intervention of Iran and Saudi-led coalition do not amount to a change of the conflict from a NIAC to IAC.

5. CONCLUSION

On the basis of the above legal analysis and its assessments, this study explicitly concludes that the conflict in Yemen still remains a NIAC and the fact that the Iran and Saudi-led coalition have intervened in support of the various parties to the conflict does not mean that the conflict has changed its nature. However, it is undisputable fact to say that Yemen conflict is vividly classified as NIAC.

BIBLIOGRAPHY

List of Books

1. Louise Arimatsu and Mohbuba Choudhury (2014), The Legal classification of the Armed Conflicts in Syria, Yemen and Libya. Page 20,
2. International Commission of Jurists, A Briefing paper (2018). Bearing the Brunt of war in Yemen: International law violations and their impact on the civilian population. Page3
3. Human Rights Watch report (2010), Yemen armed hostilities are referred to as the 'six wars'
4. Geneva Academy, Non-International Armed Conflicts in Yemen. http/www.rulac.org/browse/conlicts/non-international-armed-conflicts-in-yemen.
5. The Gulf Corperation Council Initiative (Yemen), April 2011, para.4
6. Salah, Arraf (2015), The Armed Conflict in Yemen: A complicated Mosak, Geneva Academy.

---

[37] See carswell, A. J (2009), classifying the conflict: A Soldiers dilemma.International Review of the Red Cross.

7. Derek Jinks (2013), The Temporal Scope of application of International Humanitarian Law in Contemporary Conflict. Page 2
8. carswell, A. J (2009), classifying the conflict: A Soldiers dilemma.International Review of the Red Cross.

List of cases

9. Prosecutor v. Tadic, IT-94-1, 2 October 1995, para 4341.
10. Prosecutor v. Fatmir Limaj (IT-03-66-T), 30 November 2005
11. Prosecutor v. Haradinaj (IT-04-84-T), 3 April 2008.

List of legal documents

12. The Common Article 2 of the Geneva Convention(i-iv)
13. ICRC Commentary to Article 2 of the First Geneva Convention (1952)
14. Commentary to Article 1 of Additional Protocol II.
15. The Common Article 3 of the Geneva Convention (1949)
16. UN Document in 27 March 2015, S/2015/217

ABBREVIATIONS

IHL	International Humanitarian Law
YSP	Yemeni Socialist Party
GPC	General People's Congress
LOAC	Law of Armed Conflict
IAC	International Armed Conflict
NIAC	Non-International Armed Conflict
UNSC	United Nations Security Council
UN	United Nations
CA3	Common Article 3 of Geneva Convention
CA2	Common Article 2 of Geneva Convention
APII	Addition Protocol II
ICTY	International Criminal Tribunal for the Former Yugoslavia
ICRC	International Committee of the Red Cross